Mooresville Public Library
304 South Main Street
Mooresville, NC 28115

WITHDRAWN

D1196133

Mooresville Public Library
304 South Main Street
Mooresville, NC 28115

I Can Listen

By Maria Nelson

Gareth Stevens
Publishing

Please visit our website, www.garethstevens.com. For a free color catalog of all our high-quality books, call toll free 1-800-542-2595 or fax 1-877-542-2596.

Nelson, Maria.
I can listen / by Maria Nelson.
  p. cm. — (Kids of character)
Includes index.
ISBN 978-1-4339-9030-4 (pbk.)
ISBN 978-1-4339-9031-1 (6-pack)
ISBN 978-1-4339-9029-8 (library binding)
1. Listening—Juvenile literature. I. Nelson, Maria. II. Title.
BF323.L5 N45 2014
153.68—dc23

First Edition

Published in 2014 by
Gareth Stevens Publishing
111 East 14th Street, Suite 349
New York, NY 10003

Copyright © 2014 Gareth Stevens Publishing

Designer: Nicholas Domiano
Editor: Kristen Rajczak

Photo credits: Cover, p. 1 iofoto/Shutterstock.com; p. 5 Photodisc/Thinkstock.com; pp. 7, 11 Hemera/Thinkstock.com; pp. 9, 19 iStockPhoto/Thinkstock.com; p. 13 wavebreakmedia/Shutterstock.com; p. 15 Brand X Pictures/Thinkstock.com; p. 17 Stockbyte/Thinkstock.com; p. 21 Comstock/Thinkstock.com.

All rights reserved. No part of this book may be reproduced in any form without permission in writing from the publisher, except by a reviewer.

Printed in the United States of America

CPSIA compliance information: Batch #CS13GS: For further information contact Gareth Stevens, New York, New York at 1-800-542-2595.

Contents

Boldface words appear in the glossary.

What Is Listening?

Listening is more than just hearing what someone says. Good listeners quietly pay attention to what's being said and think about it. Listening shows respect for the speaker. It takes practice and **patience**.

Listening to Learn

Maura wanted to bring a treat to school. Her mom explained each step of baking cupcakes as they worked in the kitchen. Maura listened well so she could learn something new.

Jesse's teacher was telling the class about their homework. Jesse wanted to understand something better. When the teacher finished talking, Jesse raised his hand to ask a question. He listened carefully so he would know what to do.

Sad and Happy

Gladys's feelings were hurt. She told Paulo she hadn't been **invited** to play with the other girls. Paulo was a good listener. He stayed quiet while Gladys spoke to show he cared about what she said.

Luke visited his grandparents every Sunday. They liked to tell stories about growing up in Poland. Luke didn't **interrupt**. He laughed and smiled at the funny parts to show his grandparents he enjoyed the stories. Luke listened well.

Thinking of Others

Before bed, Javier's mom always read a story to him and his sister. When she read one Javier already knew, he stayed quiet. Javier was **considerate** of his sister, who didn't know the ending. Javier was a good listener.

Elaine went to see a movie with her family. She paid attention so she could talk about it afterward. Elaine kept quiet so those around her could have a good time, too. Elaine used good listening skills.

Mei and Ravi didn't agree. Mei told Ravi what she thought and then let him talk. They took time to think before replying to what the other said. Listening well helped Ravi and Mei **communicate** better.

Showing Listening Skills

Todd was in trouble. He forgot to clean his room. While his dad talked to him, Todd made eye contact. He nodded when he understood something and answered his dad's questions. This showed that Todd was listening.

Glossary

communicate: to pass on understanding

considerate: thoughtful of the feelings of others

interrupt: to begin to talk when another person is talking

invite: to ask to go somewhere or do something

patience: the ability to wait

For More Information

Books

Burstein, John. *Have You Heard? Active Listening.* New York, NY: Crabtree Publishing Company, 2010.

Roza, Greg. *Listen Up: Knowing When and When Not to Speak.* New York, NY: Rosen Publishing, 2010.

Websites

7 Games That Sharpen Listening Skills

parentingsquad.com/7-games-that-sharpen-listening-skills
Want to be a better listener? Gather your friends and play some of these games!

Fuzzy Lion Ears

pbskids.org/lions/games/ears.html
Use your listening skills to complete words and games.

Publisher's note to educators and parents: Our editors have carefully reviewed these websites to ensure that they are suitable for students. Many websites change frequently, however, and we cannot guarantee that a site's future contents will continue to meet our high standards of quality and educational value. Be advised that students should be closely supervised whenever they access the Internet.

Index